MEET WILLIAM SHAKESPEARE

A superbly entertaining one-person play starring The Bard himself

MEET WILLIAM SHAKESPEARE

A superbly entertaining one-person play starring The Bard himself

J. Ajlouny

MEET WILLIAM SHAKESPEARE

A superbly entertaining one-person play
starring The Bard himself

Copyright © 2018, 1998
by J. Ajlouny
All rights reserved

Push Pull Press
An Imprint of:
Fresh Ink Group, LLC
Box 931
Guntersville, AL 35976
Email: info@FreshInkGroup.com
FreshInkGroup.com

Edition 1.0 1998
Edition 2.0 2018

Cover art by Anik

Performance: Any performance of this play must be licensed in writing by the publisher, including royalty arrangements. No alterations, deletions, or substitutions of a material nature may be made in this work without prior written permission of Fresh Ink Group, LLC. Authorship credit must appear on all programs and promotions in all media where space permits.

Publication: Except as permitted under the U.S. Copyright Act of 1976, no part of this publication may be reproduced, distributed, or transmitted in any form or by any means, or stored in a database or retrieval system, without prior written permission of Fresh Ink Group, LLC.

BISAC Subject Headings:
DRA010000   DRAMA / Shakespeare
PER011000   PERFORMING ARTS / Theater / General
DRA001000   DRAMA / American / General

Library of Congress Control Number: FIG will provide.

ISBN-13: 978-1-936442-73-7 Papercover
ISBN-13: 978-1-396442-79-9 Hardcover
ISBN-13: 978-1-936442-74-4 Ebooks

Dedicated to the memory of
Shakespeare scholars and
enthusiasts who have joined him
behind the big curtain in the sky

Foreword

BARD BEYOND BELIEF
The Persistent William Shakespeare Mystery

By Jonathon Bate
Professor of English Literature, University of Liverpool

The annoying thing about William Shakespeare is that his life was so mundane and so unpoetic. The only raw materials he required for the creation of his plays were a grammar school education and a lifetime in the theater as an actor, scriptwriter and shareholder of the King's Men, the most successful playing company of the age. He became the most admired dramatist of his generation, but nobody expressed any surprise when in about 1612 he handed over the role of in-house scriptwriter for the King's Men to John Fletcher and retired to his hometown of Stratford-upon-Avon, where he died quietly four years later.

Seven years after that, his fellow actors—whom he had remembered with generosity in his will— put together the sumptuous First Folio of his collection "Comedies, Histories and Tragedies." His friend Ben Jonson contributed a generous prefatory poem, "To the memory of my beloved, the author Mr.William Shakespeare," in which the "Sweet Swan of Avon" was praised as a poet who outstripped the classical authors of Greece and Rome in spite of his own somewhat limited acquaintance with their works.

Over the next hundred years, Shakespeare's reputation fluctuated, the *frenchified* court taste of the reign of Charles II showing a preference for Jonson and Fletcher. But in the course of the 18th century, first in Germany and then in England, there was a reaction against the stultifying "correctness" of French taste, with its demand for tragedy to be kept apart from comedy and high culture from low. The new watchwords were "naturalness" and "original genius" – qualities found above all in Shakespeare's plays.

By the time of the Romantic movement in the 19th century, Shakespeare had become synonymous with creative genius. But Romanticism brought a new cult of the artist's life. To be a true genius one had to live on the edge, to be struck dead like Beethoven, to be mad, bad and dangerous to know like Byron, or to wander the Orient in a drug crazed stupor like Rimbaud. So it was that a motley crue of Victorian and Edwardian eccentrics set about reinventing Shakespeare in the image of the Romantic artist.

The most enduring of these reinventions has been the attempt to dress him up as a cross between Byron and the Scarlet Pimpernel. Over the years more than a dozen Elizabethan aristocrats have been dusted off and presented to the public as the true author of the plays. Americans have been especially fascinated by the bizarre pseudo-mystery. Perhaps because the only two things the British have and Americans have not are Blue Blood and William Shakespeare, it has proved all too tempting to suppose that Shakespeare was a "nobleman in disguise."

Yet their case remains unproved. While it may seem unlikely to some, the fact remains, William Shakespeare, the Warwickshire squire, was indeed the principal author of the poems and plays attributed to him. Though the evidence to prove this fact is admittedly wanting, there is absolutely no proof that anybody other than he was the true author. Yes, many names have been submitted, ranging from Edward deVere, the 17th Earl of Oxford to Francis Bacon, and even to King James I himself. However, not only did they nor their heirs ever claim authorship, the known facts disqualify each one. The true author of Shakespeare's works was a normal family man who retired into obscurity, tended to his own affairs and enjoyed a natural death far from the madding crowds. Now that's poetic!

© 1997 Jonathon Bate
Reprinted by permission

Production History

Meet William Shakespeare enjoyed its world premiere at the Queen's Inn, Stratford, Ontario, on August 11, 1998. The first performance was a benefit for the Stratford Visitors Centre. It was produced by Barbara Ford and directed by Dan Jaroslaw. The play's U.S. premiere took place at 7th House Concert & Performance Venue in Pontiac, Michigan, on August 21, 1998, with the playwright producing and direction and stage management again by Dan Jaroslaw. Milton Papageorge starred as The Bard. It has since been produced at numerous Shakespeare Festivals and theatres in North America.

Playscript / Drama

Format: A one-person play starring an actor as William Shakespeare

Time: The present or whenever

Setting: A bare stage with a microphone and stand, a wooden chair, a table and a single spotlight. The spotlight is on and set at an angle to the floor such that its result is an elliptical circle of light. The shadows of the microphone and chair are similarly distorted by the angle of light. The table is off to the side and hosts a glass of water, a handkerchief and other accessories as required. Otherwise the stage is bare. See Prop List at the end of this script.

Action: As lights over audience dim, an appropriately attired Shakespeare enters down the center aisle from the back of the room and ascends the stage. He appears lost and confused. In his hand is a note, which he peers at with puzzlement. He toys with the microphone and discovers its function. He shrouds his eyes from the spotlight, looks around at the audience and cautiously addresses it without benet of the microphone. The action continues, much in the nature of a stand-up routine until the end, at which time the audience is invited to ask Shakespeare questions.

Audience involvement is encouraged at all times and should be freely solicited by the actor. In this regard, the action should gradually evolve from a stand-up—like performance into a Socratic-style professorial lecture.

Meet William Shakespeare

A superbly entertaining one-person play
starring The Bard himself

J. Ajlouny

The Play

Shakespeare: *Enters with skull, which has note in its mouth.*

2B or not 2B? *Scratching his head.* That is the question! *Looks at audience.* Is this the room 1B? Are you good people—perchance—seated to welcome me, William Shakespeare, of the London stage? Yes?

Good then, this must be the place. Room 2B it is.

He rips up the paper note and tosses the pieces in the air. From his vest pocket he has also removed some confetti, so that when he tosses the pieces in the air, a glimmering cascade of confetti surrounds him. The sound of a chime is also heard to signify the magical reappearance of The Bard. He surveys the stage and the room, giving the audience the clear impression that he wishes to know whom he is about to address. He then taps the microphone and carefully speaks into it:

Soft. *He stands back, clearly delighted by the result. He again approaches the microphone with glee.*

"The rain in Spain falls mainly on the plain." *He indicates his pleasure to the audience.* Yes, I wrote that one too!

By God, if we had one of these, many poor fellow's throat would have been spared inflammation. This instrument is simply marvelous, marvelous!

Very good! Let's see where shall I begin? *He ponders a moment.* I don't wish those of you in the front row to worry that I might embarrass any one of you. I'm an artist, not a cynic. I wouldn't dare call upon any one of you or otherwise single any of you out in the front of this assembly. It would be inappropriate, distasteful, no amateurish. For example, you Madam. *He selects a woman from the front row.* Will you kindly rise from your chair? I should like you to remain assured that I will in no way call attention to your relative proximity to the stage, nor your: (i.e. singular taste in clothing; unusual sense of fashion; poor judgement in the selection of a mate; etc.) This is a course gimmick employed by some novices to distract attention from themselves. I desire your attention wholeheartedly, and your respectful ear. *Playfully stern to woman.* So please lend me your ear and be of good cheer. Did you like how I made that rhyme? *Smugly.* I did that for a living, you know. Very good, you may be seated, my good lady. *He bows gracefully to her.*

Was ever a woman in this way wooed? Was ever a woman in this way won?

He pauses and looks around at the audience and clears his throat.

I was told a group of upright citizens had paid ready funds to me. And that they would be awaiting my arrival at this hour in room 2B. Now that we've settled that I am he, that this is the place, and that you are the citizens, I see no reason why we should not proceed. *To audience.* Agreed?

He demands a verbal response from the audience.

Let me commence with a preemptory remark concerning my unease with speaking about myself. As an actor, a trade by the way which I frankly never especially enjoyed, I was trained to assume the identities of countless others. It's great fun, really, but it does tend to wear one's own sense of identity away, somewhat. I have, on more than one occasion, actually forgotten who I am supposed to be. Ironically, my true, private self has never failed to assert itself except whilst I am upon the stage. And as you no doubt realize by now, the whole world's a damn stage. So if you will permit me to momentarily forget that I am presently upon this platform, I would like to share with you certain personal reminiscences and anecdotes about which you may not otherwise read in one of those fallacious biographies about me.

He positions his chair and takes a seat upon it. He pulls a packet of cards from his breast pocket.

Oh yes, I have one other matter to address. I have been given a list of questions by the management to answer. I think they feared I could not proceed without a script of some kind in hand. For now then, let their fears be banished. *Pauses.* Would that be banished or banish'd? *To himself.* "For now then, let their fears be banish'd." *He crosses to the table, takes up his plume and scribbles out the line.* Ah yes, perfect iambic pentameter: banish'd it is! Can anyone tell me why Elizabethan writers such as myself wrote in iambic pentameter?

Well, first of all, this particular metrical pattern, te dum, de dum, te dum is the pattern that most resembles our own English speech. Many of you probably speak in such patterns on a regular basis but are unaware of it. But most importantly, can anyone tell me what this metrical pattern most closely represents? Te dum, de dum, te dum? *He points to an audience member.*

That's correct! The beating of our hearts. And you thought you wouldn't learn anything today, didn't you sir?

Enough said. Let their fears be banish'd. I will begin exactly where I should begin: At the beginning. And I will end exactly where I should end: When the audience has had quite enough!

Who was it who said brevity is the soul of wit? *He laughs and enjoys a drink.*

Let's see...oh yes...I was born in the market town of Stratford, a smallish hamlet in the countryside of the county of Warwickshire in 1564. Stratford is situated upon the banks of the river Avon, which is itself a healthy stretch of water, even in the summertime. Thus the common name: Stratford-upon-Avon. To the north by a distance of twenty-five miles is the city of Coventry. Scattered between us and in all other directions, are a number of smaller towns and villages, and the chief occupation of the region is, as you might expect, farming. Here and there along the beauteous English landscape are situated several great estates, or halls as we refer to them. It was not uncommon that these halls would play host to members of the royal court, and indeed, from time to time, to the Queen herself, and her entire retinue. This could be an occasion of either great good fortune or impending disaster, depending upon how long Her Majesty suffered to remain in residence there. You see, in the later years of her reign, her purse was such that it behooved her to accept the hospitality and generosity of her many nobles, thereby saving her the trouble and the expense of setting up her court in any one of her own great residences. Clever woman, she was! It was from Her Majesty I observed that few people suffer from want of tact. For most it's a pleasure. After her departure from this world she was remembered by all, but most especially by her many creditors. *He laughs hardily.*

But getting back to Stratford. Well, there isn't much to say, really. My childhood was not unlike that of any other child in the town. Owing to my father's relative success in business and civic affairs, I was enrolled in the King's New School. It was there that I first learned about books, and was inspired to reading by the headmaster there, a wily and witty man whose gentle manner and rustic humor I will ever be grateful to have enjoyed. It was a shame he was ousted from his position for stealing three bottles of wine, especially after having survived allegations that he seduced the daughter of one of Stratford's leading citizens. Oh what a work of art is man! I suppose it was he who revealed to me that all men are fools in part. For what is a fool except an otherwise upstanding man making a momentary mistake of judgement? Nature seldom makes a fool. She simply furnishes us with the opportunity to do it ourselves.

> *"Wit...put me into good fooling. Those wits, that think they have thee, do very oft' prove fools; and I, that I am sure I lack thee, may pass for a wise man..."*
>
> (Feste from Twelfth Night; A1 S5)

He sits and gets comfortable.

But of course you are most interested in how my life and the rise of the theatre converged. My earliest recollection involving the theatre was when I was but five years of age. At that time my father Jon Shakespeare, son of Richard, was our town's High Bailiff, the mayor, if you will. It was in this capacity that he was frequently asked to sit in judgement of the works of any one of several touring acting companies, or players as we referred to them, for the purpose of granting (or denying) a license permitting them to hold performances in the town's jurisdiction. In those days, you see, a troupe was subject to confiscation—unless their presentations were sanctioned by the authorities. For this purpose, most of the better troupes sought the patronage of peers to endorse them. Having such a patent was the only way to steer clear of the chief censor of the day, the Master of Revels, who worked directly for the Queen's chief counselor, Lord Burleigh. But I digress. Suffice it to say, it was during these review performances, that the world of the theatre and the art of acting was introduced to me. Honestly. Just that simple.

He looks up and away from his chair.

Oh father, if you only knew what chain of events you set in motion. What voices you liberated by letting me tag along.

Not only did I get to see a variety of shows, most of them being comedies or passion plays, but most importantly, I got to meet the players themselves. Among the players I had occasion to meet were the Earl of Warwick's Men, the Earl of Leicester's Men and those of the Earl of Pembroke, who were my particular favorites.

Being an impressionable young lad, as I dare say most are at that age, I was taken with enthusiasm for, of all things, swords and spears and halberds and of battle cries, trumpets blaring and the like. War, I guess we call it. And with blood and guts and gore and such, just like little boys often are. *He picks up the stick cane.* As I look back, I realize my fascination was fixed by my having had the opportunity to help carry the theatrical props to and from the troupe's wagons. I had never held a sword before. But that first time made all the difference to me. From then on, any stick that could be sharpened was my friend.

And the stage was set, so to speak. From then afterwards, I, along with my friends, and my younger brothers Gilbert and Richard, considered ourselves as Stratford's very own defense force. With our imaginations thus set ablaze, all of us became hooked on things theatrical. It was really just that simple. But not a one of us imagined making a career in the theatre. Indeed, the very concept was virtually unknown to us in those days. Theatre, as a distinct form of art, was but in its infancy during my youth. Our only introduction to drama was in our classrooms during Greek and Latin instruction. As you imagine, such studies were of little interest to young country lads with a territory to defend!

> **Once more unto the breach, dear friends, once more, Or close the wall up with our English dead!**
>
> *(King Henry from Henry V; A3 S1)*

He lunges forward with the sword and strains himself. He rises and walks around the stage to collect his thoughts before proceeding.

Let me conveniently skip over the next several of years. For life in Stratford was generally uneventful, and frankly, I don't remember much of it. Childhood was for me a happy time, and though it was hard at times, and death was a constant reminder of our own mortality, we got on reasonably well. For this I owe most to my mother Mary. Her love and genuine goodness was not lost on us children. As a matter of fact, it was with her family relations from the nearby village of Wilmcotte that we children enjoyed our greatest adventures. It was on those streets and in those fields that the world introduced itself to me. I suppose the wide eyes and shapely figure of my cousin Charlotte had something to do with it as well. It was with her that I first sampled, what I have ever hence called "the emotion of loving." And it was with her also that I first experienced the physical element of love, if you know what I mean. Ah, Charlotte, beauty is thy name.

Quoting Biron in Love's Labours Lost:

"For where is any author in the world,

Teaches such beauty as a woman's eye?"

Ah, so true, so true. But of course I believe it's true, I wrote it! Didn't I?

Owing to the onset of my father's sudden bout of distemper, I left school at age 13 and commenced working with him and my uncle Thomas sewing gloves and fashioning clothes of cotton, linen and leather. I was to be apprenticed as such, until their money loaning losses caused us some dire financial embarrassment. The next time you read *Hamlet*, when you come across Polonius' advice to his son

Laertes, I think you will now better understand why I wrote the words: "Neither a borrower nor a lender be. For loan oft' loses both itself and friend." I was let go and forced to fend for myself as a laborer in the fields around our town. A laborer! Can you imagine? No, no, no. These hands were made for finer things than a shovel, I can assure you of that ladies and gentlemen. It was not the life for me. *Aside.* You see, I was blessed (or cursed) with a delicate constitution.

In the summer of 1581, when I was but 17 years of age, a remarkable event occurred. This was the jubilee festival at Kenilworth Hall, a great building of turrets and towers, which was the estate of the Earl of Leicester. It wasn't the event of the season but of the decade! Assembled there for almost thirty-five days was a fair so grand, and engagements so thrilling—music, theatre, fireworks and the like—that I stole away to work among them without the knowledge or permission of my father. It was a good decision. For it was at the festival that I once again entered the world of performance, the land of make-believe. At age 17, I was unexpectedly hired on as a voice prompter to the Earl's Men. And when, having suffered the destruction of their many scripts during a heavy rainfall, I had occasion to re-write them, they doubled my wages.

He stands.

So impressed were they by the neatness of my hand, and by the suggestions I offered as to this scene and that dialogue, I found myself encouraged to remain with them for the extent of their travels to Coventry and Bristol. What a thrill! And the remuneration I was offered was more than three-times that I was earning on the land. Imagine that. My father and mother were skeptical at first but eventually permitted me to go with them…after I gave them all my earnings. As it turned out, their fears about the general degeneracy of the players and their taggers-on was entirely…well founded. They were a motley crew, to be sure. These men and some boys acted in roles, they did not model them. I could fill you with many delightful and dreadful tales of my experiences with them, but this is supposed to be a family show, so I dare not. *Whispers.* Timing is everything.

But like all good things, my touring came to an end. My experiences with the Earl's Men, though rewarding for me, were quickly forgotten once I returned to life in Stratford. Father's position improved somewhat, and this was a relief, but my personal fortunes looked as bleak as the next fellow's. London was the place to be. But for us in the countryside, London was a world away.

He sits.

I'll skip over the circumstances of my marriage and the birth of my daughter Susanna. These events happened so quickly, as if by accident, that I have yet to fully comprehend them myself. Indeed, it is difficult to understand how a handsome young dowdy as myself should be forced by circumstances to marry a woman eight years his senior due to circumstances beyond his intentions. Yet, it happened, and thus I feared at the age of 18, my life was over before it had really begun. At least it seemed so to me.

Oh, Anne was tolerable in her own way, I suppose, but I never liked her much. Anne, you see, suffered from an extreme case of indiscretion. She was the town gossip. The only way to get her attention was to tell her to mind her own business. (I always thought she'd make a great understudy for a mocking bird!) One of the things that really miffed me about her is the way in which she picked through my pockets and bags at night. This, my friends, was the extent of my wife's feminine touch! I can tell you that. The only thing I really ever learned from her was the kind of husband she preferred! Had I not been rejected by Charlotte I'm quite sure I never would have laid a hand on her. *He closes his eyes, leans his head back and smiles as he recalls her beauty.*

> *"Thou art as tyrannous, so as thou art,*
>
> *As those whose beauties proudly make them cruel.*
>
> *For well thou know'st to my dear doting heart,*
>
> *Thou art the fairest and most precious jewel."*
>
> *(First stanza of Sonnet 131)*

Consequently, directly after our wedding, which was hastily arranged, my entire being concentrated on one thing and one thing only: How to get the hell out of Stratford and down to Londontown.

He springs to his feet.

The first opportunity came almost five years later. Five years! By that time there were three children in our nest, two girls and a son she named Hamnet. *Loudly.* Hamnet! Oh my friends, I tell you she must have done this to provoke me! Being an observant member of the Church of England, I don't believe in reincarnation. But if I ever come back as a dog I fear Anne would come back as a flea! Living in my father's house, with my brothers and sisters and my own family was less than ideal for a restless spirit such as mine. And the circumstances in which I found myself entrapped peaked in yearning and wanderlust. So finding a way out of there was my singular preoccupation. What I needed was a horse. I would have traded my wife for a horse! *(He grabs the foil and stoops ala Richard III.)* A horse! A horse, my wife for a horse! *(To audience.)* Well I suppose it's a bit more dramatic if I had a large hump on my back, a withered left arm, a crooked nose and was under siege by the Earl of Richmond.

He mimes sword-play.

I think it aptly demonstrates exactly how desperate I was at the time! *He laughs and pauses with a drink.*

Now, can anyone tell me what finally facilitated my escape? Anyone?

It was the theatre, of course! The stage literally rescued me from the dull routine of existence. In the spring of 1587 the Lord Strange's Men came to Stratford to set up for a week. I recall hearing their wagon pageant on the road to town. It rolled over Clopton Bridge led by a team of four white horses? (Or was it a pack-horse and a few mules? I can't recall with specificity.) I dropped everything and caught up with them just as they reached the High Street. Imagine my surprise to find among them several of the friends I had made some years before with the Earl's Men. So glad were we to see one another that we laughed for what seemed like hours. Those were the good old days. Though such days are made more grand due to the vagaries of memory, I recall our reunion with such delight it fails to light a flame in my spirit. Well...I fell in with them... and didn't leave them for over twenty years!

He arises once again, enjoys a drink and stretches his legs.

Tempo picks up.

The road to London was a long and dusty one. Or was it rutted and muddy? Well, I can't remember, but either way it wasn't particularly pleasurable. We could tell we were getting near the city walls when we started passing throngs of people on the sides of the road. And soon we saw masses of humanity, more than I ever imagined lived in all of England. They were mostly poor and decrepit creatures but going about their business like man always has and always will.

London itself was amazing to me. It seemed like a thousand Stratfords and a hundred Coventrys all packed into one endless swirl of streets and buildings. I think it is the noise of the city that I will remember most distinctly. It was as loud as a battlefield, and at times, nearly as dangerous. When we entered the city through Newgate, we were subjected to inspection. But a few bottles of wine and some cheese were all we needed to make the requisite impression. In so passing, I felt certain I was passing into a new life; a new world! *He sprinkles more confetti and the chime is once again heard.* I was not wrong!

Over the next three years, however, I gained some significant experience in theatrical circles. When we were not running from the law, we were running from our creditors. It was a hectic existence, but I enjoyed every hour of it. It certainly beat the pace of life in the countryside.

In times of distress and loneliness, however, I thought of my days in Stratford. It tended to cheer me up. But I'll admit I was not tempted to return. Not even for a visit. London was everything one could imagine and more. It was a bouquet of contradictions, well-ordered and chaotic, clean and filthy, welcoming and hostile, promising and depressing my friends. Every day in the city of London was an adventure. For me it was a time of awakening and curiosity. Yes, curiosity most of all.

He pours himself another glass of wine and drinks it in a single gulp.

I had the good fortune of meeting the writer Christopher Marlowe when he was attached to the Earl of Pembroke's Men. It was with him that I polished my skills in crafting scripts, editing dialogue and staging productions. It was also he who introduced me to Mr. James Burbage, a prominent actor who had built his own theatre, called simply The Theatre, in the north of London, outside the city walls…and beyond the watchful eyes of the city authorities.

It was under the tutelage of Burbage and his sons Richard and Cuthbert that my first self-penned plays were performed. *He looks at the same woman in the audience with whom he toyed with at the beginning of the play and winks at her.* Did you like that one? *With emphasis to the point of almost spitting.* "Self-penned plays were performed!" *To an audience member.* There is plenty more where that came from, I assure you Madame.

You see, at the time there was a fierce competition among the rival theatres for audiences, especially for recognition and patronage from nobles and other highborn Londoners. The problem was the relative few scripts available to perform. England, you see, had no tradition of playwriting. All scripts that were available at the time were controlled by the rival companies. It made sense, therefore, for the Burbages to commission their own scripts. So they could own them. Thankfully, they had confidence in my abilities to create for them the kind of theatrical entertainment they determined was best suited for the patrons they sought to attract.

Not being an educated man, nor very experienced for that matter, I gathered up what stories I could and began re-telling them in a manner suited for our audiences. I began with an account of the Roman general Titus Andronicus, a story I particularly enjoyed, because it was gruesome and violent. I knew our patrons would enjoy it as well. Spectators of the day, you see, were conditioned to expect plenty of violence and gore. I think you understand, and I don't imagine human nature has changed much in the ensuing years. After all, the only real competition the theatres faced was from the several bull and bear baiting rings situated on the south banks of the Thames. In those rings, vicious hounds were unleashed upon chained beasts who had been plucked from the wilds. They were mauled and gnawed apart to the frightful glee of the spectators. So in giving them the horrific torture and murder scenes in *Titus*, I was but catering to the preference of the audience. I see little harm in that.

Thankfully, however, I followed it with a lighter piece, *The Comedy of Errors*, based upon two stories by the Roman playwright Plautus. You may know it as *The Brothers Menaechmus*. This was a measured *response* to the concerns of good taste and moral values than being espoused by the Master of Revels and other local officials whose sensitivities were so easily aroused, and apparently, offended. While neither play was particularly popular nor profitable. But we made enough to keep going, so the rush was on for more scripts. I was more than happy to oblige my employers. And the wages were very good indeed!

My next work...*to the audience*...don't worry sir/madam, I'm not going to go through all 37 of them.

What followed was the trilogy of plays based upon the life and times of King Henry VI. (Or Prince Hal as you may know him.) This was James Burbage's idea, not mine. He felt a political drama showing a triumphant England would be, well let's just say, useful. I relied largely upon the events related in Raphael Holinshed's *Chronicles*, which were published just five or so years before. I gave him a what I thought he wanted, and again it was well received. The fact that we made three separate plays out of the story was a testament to Burbage's brilliant business acumen. *(He winks at the same woman in the audience.)* He said, "Will, why sell just one ticket when we could sell three separate ones." A clever man, he was. A clever (and shrewd) man indeed!

Natural pause.

And you needed to be clever in those days just to survive. It was not easy, no! The greatest resistance we faced was within the halls of Parliament, where certain Puritans, as they came to be known, condemned the theatre as a breeding ground for degenerates, thieves, drunkards and most notably, atheists. Local church authorities agreed and supported efforts to regulate the content and manner of performances. Under such conditions, finding plays to satisfy the prevailing moods was not an easy task.

Like all good art, playwriting is very hard work. Look at any of the great masterpieces of the world, from the sculpture of the ancients to the painting of the Renaissance masters. There is nothing simple or easy about their work. Real art requires painstaking determination. And for me, the harder I worked at my writing the better it became. This was especially true of the so-called comedies. What is humor, anyway? I've always thought a sense of humor is what makes you want to laugh at something you'd be angry about if it happened to you.

He descends the stage and enters the audience.

Stagecraft you see, is a curious thing. The theatre is a universe in which all things are possible. These possibilities scare some and delight others. Finding a happy medium was always first and foremost upon my mind. It was for this purpose that I tended to write a history, followed by a comedy, which in turn was followed by a tragedy. We had to keep our productions varied to keep our patrons entertained…and our critics off their guards. And for the most part, it worked!

He selects a gentleman from the audience.

Can you tell me what other obstacle we neophyte players were forced to contend with as well? Anybody?

Well, as if the prevailing hostilities weren't enough, there was one more obstacle we neophyte players had to contend with. This was the terrible outbreak of bubonic fever. The Plague, you see, was always a threat to our well-being. And in 1592, just as things seemed to be going our way, a woeful bout of plague descended upon the city, and consequently all the theatres and other places of public assembly were ordered closed.

My colleagues chose to hit the road. I chose to remain in London and seek the patronage of a noble to enable me to pursue my writing. I won't bore you with the details of how I eventually accomplished this (because I don't wish to embarrass myself) but suffice it to say I did so, rather successfully. And how could I have done better than obtaining the support of Henry Wriothesely, the Second Earl of Southhampton? This fine young gentleman was the heir to a substantial fortune, and a ward of the Queen. It was under his patronage that I penned the two lyrical poems *Venus and Adonis* and *The Rape of Lucrece*. It was my public recitation of these poems in many great estates that finally established me as a poet and reader of some repute. Please understand, ladies and gentlemen, poetry, for me, is the language of the unconscious. It is the unmined lode of all our thoughts and desires, the faint voice from within that yearns to be heard. The ability to hear that voice is what all poets hold in common.

> *"The poet's eye, in a fine frenzy rolling,*
> *Doth glance from heaven and earth, from earth to heaven;*
> *And as imagination bodies forth*
> *The forms of things unknown,*
> *The poet's pen turns them to shapes and gives to airy nothing*
> *A local habitation and a name."*
>
> *(Theseus from A Midsummer Night's Dream; A5 S1)*

Yet, I have not previously mentioned the anger my works evoked in certain quarters, have I? And to understand the position I achieved, I would be remiss not describing it in passing. For not only did we players face personal, practical and financial difficulties, and not forgetting the suspicion the authorities held us under, I was personally by more than one critic in the university community. An upstart crow, that's what they called me. An upstart crow. Damn that Robert Greene. *Quoting.* "Mister Shakespeare is ill-fit to write anything of literary merit."

That I was not high-born nor well-bred seems to have engendered in these parties no shortage of hostility, nay, rage, against me. *Pauses.* Well, I persevered. But by the close of 1594, I had succeeded in vanquishing all doubt.

Frankly, I would have preferred to hack my critics apart with a sword from our prop inventory. But it was my pen that silenced them, and eventually won them over such that I became the most celebrated playmaker in London. Ironic, isn't it, how the pen is more mighty than the sword.

With the theatres once again available to perform in, I and my players, who by this time had become the servants of the Lord Chamberlain—no small feat at that—embarked on a singular adventure in the theatre. Over the period of the next ten years we churned out perhaps two dozen or so new presentations, all too much public approbation. We played at court, in great estates, on the road in town squares and in inn-yards near and far. The pace was not an easy one, mind you, but our enterprise was relatively successful both critically and financially. Had it not been for the pain I developed in my right hand, and in my backside, I might have written another ten or so plays, maybe more, who knows?

He returns to the stage. Takes a drink of water. Surveys the audience once again, and continues.

Back in Stratford, things were going well for my family. My father's fortunes improved such that he and my uncle Thomas were awarded a coat of arms from the Lord Lyon on behalf of Her Majesty. This was a great occasion and the cause for a happy celebration in our household. Even Anne managed a smile on occasion. But our joy was soon ended. Our son Hamnet, but ten years old and the very definition of a perfect son, died of fever. I became inconsolable. For I had barely known my son.

I learned a sadness then, a sadness buoyed by shame, that ever afterward I kept deep within my heart. The mournful expression of that sadness can be heard, often enough I imagine, in the tragedies *Lear* and *Macbeth*, and in other places in my characters, to be sure. After all, what does a writer write about, if not about himself.

> **"Grief fills the room up of my absent child,**
>
> **Lies in his bed, walks up and down with me,**
>
> **Puts on his pretty looks, repeats his words,**
>
> **Stuffs out his vacant garments with his form;**
>
> **Then have I reason to be fond of grief."**
>
> *(Constance from King John; A2 S1)*

He slowly collects himself.

"A heavy heart hath not a nimble tongue."

Ladies and gentlemen, I will close presently. Permit me now to note a few additional events I would be remiss in not describing, if ever so briefly. Let's see...oh yes...The Globe! The Globe!

Well, our company of players wisely invested in a theatre of our own, which we called The Globe. It was located on the south bank of the river, not far from the London Bridge but perhaps too close to the prison we called facetiously, The Globe was opened in 1599. Our first play there was my rendition of the story of *Julius Caesar*. We met with much success there, so much so that I was able to invest my earnings in land and houses in Stratford. Indeed, I was supporting my entire family, and what at times felt like half the residents of the town.

> *"O the fierce wretchedness that glory brings us!*
> *Who would not wish to be from wealth exempt,*
> *Since riches point to misery and contempt."*
>
> (Flavius from Timon of Athens; A4 S2)

Let's see...what else? Ah yes, the death of Her Majesty Queen Elizabeth at the beginning of 1603 was an event of great importance.

And frankly it didn't come too soon. In the last several years of her reign we suffered war with Spain, rebellion in Ireland, insurrection at home and a period of extended depression and poverty. With the arrival of King James of Scotland in March 1603, however, the situation noticeably improved. I and my fellows were made, by royal patent, the King's very own Men. It was the crowning achievement of our careers. Imagine, a young lad from Stratford all those years ago was now performing in the service of the King in palace and hall. It was a privilege I can scarce believe I was worthy of. Back in Stratford, the news was well-received. Soon I was known as Square William. What a lark! *He laughs loudly and repeats the title.*

He paces back and forth.

I befriended other notable writers, most closely Messrs. Ben Jonson and Thomas Nashe. You know what they say about keeping your friends close but your enemies even close. I could not countenance the rivalry of this pair, and I and my fellows did much to frustrate their purposes. It was shameful but nonetheless required at the time. We had a business to protect and that's exactly what we did. Oh, in time we made our peace but while we were in the thick of battle we fought hard and we fought well!

> "In peace, there's nothing so becomes a man
> As modest stillness and humility:
> But when the blast of war blows in our ears,
> Then imitate the action of the tiger;
> Stiffen the sinews, summon up the blood,
> Disguise faire nature with hard favored rage!"
>
> *(King Henry from Henry V; A3 S1)*

I suppose we could have continued the frantic pace we set for ourselves, especially after we leased the old Blackfriars monastery as our winter stage in 1608. But by then I was tired, and frankly, rather bored, (as I fear you are now). I penned *Coriolanus*, *Cymbeline*, *The Winter's Tale* and *The Tempest* in this period, among others. By 1611, I was spent. I therefore resolved to return to Stratford to live out the remainder of my life among my family. The Men continued to pay me for the use of my plays, and

I was content. It was only after the accidental destruction of The Globe in 1613 (due to a fire during the premiere of *King Henry VIII*) that I withdrew from the theatre completely and returned to Stratford. I decided I had enough of the life in London and of the stage. Who was it who said, "All the world's a stage?"

Now good friends, I've spoken long enough. It is possible to say too much, even about the most fascinating subjects. I trust you have found my remarks both enlightening and amusing. I came into this world as a simple country lad. I exited as a successful man of some accomplishment. Might it not be more interesting if I refrain from saying more except about that which you may be curious?

Do any of you have a question to ask or a comment you'd like to offer? Now is your chance. I fear that in a short time I will be too tired to proceed, so please unburden yourselves freely…and in quick order.

Who will be first? You sir? Madam, you?

The play concludes following the Q & A section with;

Conclusion.

He stands.

Now dear friends, you must permit me to conclude this immodest presentation, the story of my life and the particular accidents gone by since I came unto this island. *(Gestures to stage.)* For this one night/day, which part of it I wasted with such discourse as I doubt not made it go quick away, is now at an end.

Farewell and good evening/day to you all.

He bows graciously.

Finis.

Sample Questions and Answers

"Where did you get the idea to write...?"

I never had any ideas except for those that were offered to me by circumstance. All of my works are based upon ancient fables or medieval tales that most people were acquainted with to some extent. Thus I could be original without being too daring, if you will. English audiences are a cantankerous bunch, you see, not nearly as well behaved or as accepting as yourselves. And if you gave them something foreign to their understanding they might react violently. So for purposes of self-preservation I never strayed too far from what was familiar to them.

"How many brothers and sisters did you have?"

My mother gave birth to eight children, four boys and four girls. I was the eldest son and owing to the premature deaths of my two older sisters, the eldest child. However, only my younger sister Joan and I married and had families of our own. Brother Gilbert stayed home and managed our Stratford affairs with father. Brothers Richard and Edmund followed me to

London and took up with us in the theatre. But neither prospered there and so both returned to Stratford where they passed on. My father lived a good long life, as did my mother. They, more than I, knew the pain of surviving their children. They were good people and I'm happy they were my parents.

"How did you write so many plays?"

I had little choice, really. We were actors and needed plays in which to act. As nobody else offered to write anything for us, the task was left to me. You see, we had to perform as many as five plays in a single week. Since the audience at that time was limited to those who dared to come and see us, we were forced to offer them new plays all the time or they might stop attending. So you see, I had little choice. That's why I wrote over a dozen comedies when I would have preferred to write just two or three.

"Which play is your favorite?"

That's like asking a father which is his favorite child. I can't do it. Which is yours?

"How did you write so many famous lines?"

Well, they weren't famous when I wrote them so I really can't tell you. As a matter of literary craftsmanship, I always believed that short and succinct was best. Brevity is the soul of wit, I've always said. My plays would have been a might bit shorter had I not been writing for actors. They demanded the long speeches, not the audiences. "More matter, less art," Richard Burbage was often heard to cry. So I gave him what he wanted. *Hamlet* was written especially for him, you know. I did my best to trip him up, but he was too good. A marvelous actor he was, as were my other fellows. Absolutely marvelous!

"To what do you account your deep understanding of human nature?"

I gave the subject a great deal of thought!

"Did you ever imagine you would become the most popular writer in history?"

I never gave that any thought!

"Did you ever imagine you would have such a great influence on the English language?"

This question presumes I have. I don't know, have I? I wrote to the best of my ability. Some of my works give me great pride. Others are an embarrassment to me. The extent to which

I was influential with the language is uncertain to me. I suppose anybody who wrote as prolifically as I did at a time when writing as a profession was something entirely new might have been as influential as I'm claimed to have been. I don't believe I wrote with any special purpose in mind other than to support my fellows and entertain my audiences. The poetry is, of course, especially the sonnets, an exception.

"Who is the Dark Lady in your later sonnets?"

Wouldn't you like to know! All I will say on this subject is that her identity remains a secret, despite the foolish meddling of so many so-called scholars. Even Professor Rowse got it wrong, though he went to the grave believing he cracked the mystery. The Sonnets were written on communication. They were written to tease and amuse. While I believe they are, on the whole, excellent examples of the form, it is but indulgence to de-construct them.

"Do you consider yourself a poet or a playwright?"

Let me ask you: Which do you consider me to be?

I am and always only ever tried to be a man who attempted to express what he thought needed to be said. I thank God for giving me the ability to do it. More I cannot say.

"Many scholars have attempted to prove you are gay. Are you?"

I think I am…most of the time anyway. To be sad is a sorry state. Not even our Savior was without his mirth.

"Did you see the movie 'Shakespeare In Love'?"

What movie? I've always been in love; in love with life, with language, with leisure, and of course, with alliteration.

About J. Ajlouny

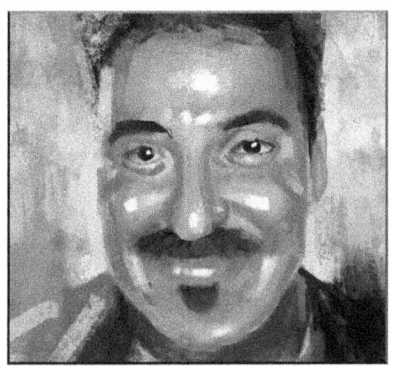

Playwright J. Ajlouny is an attorney, agent, and writer from Detroit. His many plays include *The Trial of William Shakespeare*, *The Red Poppy: Joseph Stalin at Home*, and *Marilyn, Norma Jean and Me*. He is also the author of more than a dozen humor and popular reference books under the pen name Joey West. Joseph is director of The Federal Bureau of Entertainment, a production company that specializes in the development and presentation of solo theatre plays and musical reviews.

Prop List

1. An authentic period man's costume
2. Feather quill and charred paper
3. Confetti/glittering dust
4. Chime cue
5. Pitcher and goblet
6. Table with period accessories
7. Skull
8. Stick cane
9. Foil/rapier
10. Chair and rug
11. Note paper and note cards

Tech Requirements

1. Microphone and stand.
2. Sound cue tape of chime
3. Audio player
4. Standard lighting

Fresh Ink Group
Independent Publisher

Imprint: Fresh Ink Group
Imprint: Push Pull Press

✥

Hardcovers
Softcovers
All Ebook Platforms
Worldwide Distribution

✥

Indie Author Services
Book Development, Editing, Proofing
Graphic/Cover Design
Video/Trailer Production
Website Creation
Social Media Management
Writing Contests
Writers' Blogs
Podcasts

✥

Authors
Editors
Artists
Experts
Professionals

✥

FreshInkGroup.com
Email: info@FreshInkGroup.com
Twitter: @FreshInkGroup
Google+: Fresh Ink Group
Facebook.com/FreshInkGroup
LinkedIn: Fresh Ink Group

Fresh Ink Group
Guntersville

THE TRIAL OF WILLIAM SHAKESPEARE

Few men have endured the indignity of having their very existence challenged as thoroughly as William Shakespeare, late of Stratford-upon-Avon. From scholars to amateur enthusiasts, many cannot bring themselves to believe he wrote his own body of work. Playwright J. Ajlouny presents the arguments for and against, all statements and proofs drawn from the historical record. Everybody must decide for himself, but *The Trial of William Shakespeare* makes the controversy both intriguing and fun.

Push Pull Press/Fresh Ink Group

Marilyn, Norma Jean and Me

In this boisterous but sensitive drama, playwright J. Ajlouny looks beyond public image to find the heart of this young woman thrust wildly into fame as a sex symbol. Presented as a play-in-the-making within a play, *Marilyn, Norma Jean and Me* weaves biography with humor to explore the movie star's widely speculated desire to leave Hollywood for Broadway. The author imagines her innocence and vulnerability, her friendliness and loyalty, even as the public image threatens to steal her humanity. This play is a masterpiece, not just because it is so good, but for its powerful way of finding the real Norma Jean in the legend known as Marilyn Monroe.

PUSH PULL PRESS / Fresh Ink Group

Who Said That?

Who Said That? provides an entertaining and authoritative reference for the origins and meanings of our common figures of speech.

- Who said 100+ famous expressions?
- Who *really* said them?
- What did they actually say?
- What did they actually mean?
- Why did they say them that way?
- Who repeated what was said?

Surprisingly true, sometimes strange, always fascinating, the stories about whence came these expressions will entertain, educate, and even amaze you.

Fresh Ink Group

Figuratively Speaking

A "Figure of speech" is an expression that creates a more forceful or dramatic meaning, such as "stretch the truth" or "baptism by fire." We finally have a thesaurus to discover their origins and the sources of their meanings. Whether reading it for fun, researching phrases you use, or studying the symbolic foundations of our language, Figuratively Speaking is the resource you'll reach for time and again.

Fresh Ink Group

Adventures in Leninland

Prior to the collapse of Communism and the break-up of the Eastern-bloc empire of the U.S.S.R., a humorist and fledgling Kremlinologist was invited to tour the vast Red Landscape. Along the rails and roads traveled, he met a cast of colorful characters and faced a host of bizarre situations that only such a world can produce. These stories and essays portray a few of the fascinating, tragic, and whimsical things he discovered.

Fresh Ink Group

www.ingramcontent.com/pod-product-compliance
Lightning Source LLC
Chambersburg PA
CBHW061249040426
42444CB00010B/2311